Living Things and Their Young

FOLLETT FAMILY LIFE EDUCATION PROGRAM

Living Things and Their Young

Julian May

Follett Publishing Company   Chicago   New York

Photographic Credits

Cover picture and title pages by Black Star

Black Star, 9 right; Allen Carr, 6 top and bottom, 7 left and right; Ben Dennison, 38 left and right, 39, 46, 47 top and bottom; Freelance Photographers Guild, Inc., 8, 26 top; E. Grave, Photo Researchers, Inc., 10 top right and bottom right; Grant Heilman, Agricultural Photography, 9 top and left, 43; International Pacific Salmon Fisheries Commission, New Westminster, B.C., Canada, 18, 23, 24 top and bottom; R. Jaques, Photo Researchers, Inc., 26 bottom right; R. Kinne, Photo Researchers, Inc., 16, 42; Hille Kleinstra from Shostal, 41 left; Tom McHugh, Photo Researchers, Inc., 40; J. Monroe, Photo Researchers, Inc., 20; Roger Rutter, Vanides Design, 41 right; Dr. Roman Vishniac, 10 left, 13, 14 left

Illustrations by Don Meighan

Designed by Chestnut House

Copyright © 1969 by Follett Publishing Company. All rights reserved. No part of this book may be reproduced in any form without written permission from the publisher. Manufactured in the United States of America. Published simultaneously in Canada by The Ryerson Press, Toronto.

Standard Book Number 695-85294-9   Trade Binding
Standard Book Number 695-45294-0   Library Binding
Standard Book Number 695-25294-1   Educational Binding

Library of Congress Catalog Card Number: 68-10481

First Printing A

Consultants

John G. Chaltas
Associate Professor of Education
University of New Hampshire
formerly Director of Instruction
Glencoe, Illinois Public Schools

Tess Cogen
Family Life Educator
formerly Director, Family Life Education
The Association for Family Living

Willard Z. Kerman, M.D.
Pediatrician
Past Member and President
Glencoe, Illinois Board of Education

Curtis C. Melnick
Associate Superintendent
Chicago Public Schools

Edward Victor
Professor of Science Education
Northwestern University

Trilobite, Cambrian Era: Utah

Fern, Pennsylvanian Age: Illinois

These fossils show us how some living things looked long ago.

Bony fish, Cretaceous Age: Wyoming

Coral, Silurian Age: Michigan

No one is sure just how the first living thing appeared on earth.

It was probably very small, floating in the warm ocean that covered the world billions of years ago.

It probably looked a lot like the non-living matter around it. But there was a difference. The living thing could make other living things just like itself.

It could REPRODUCE.

African elephant

In today's world, as far as we know, only living things can make other living things. Life does not appear all by itself. Life comes from other life.

This is called REPRODUCTION.

Muscovy duck

Thompson's gazelle

Thoroughbred mare and colt

These are all one-celled living things.

Diatom

Stentor

Paramecium

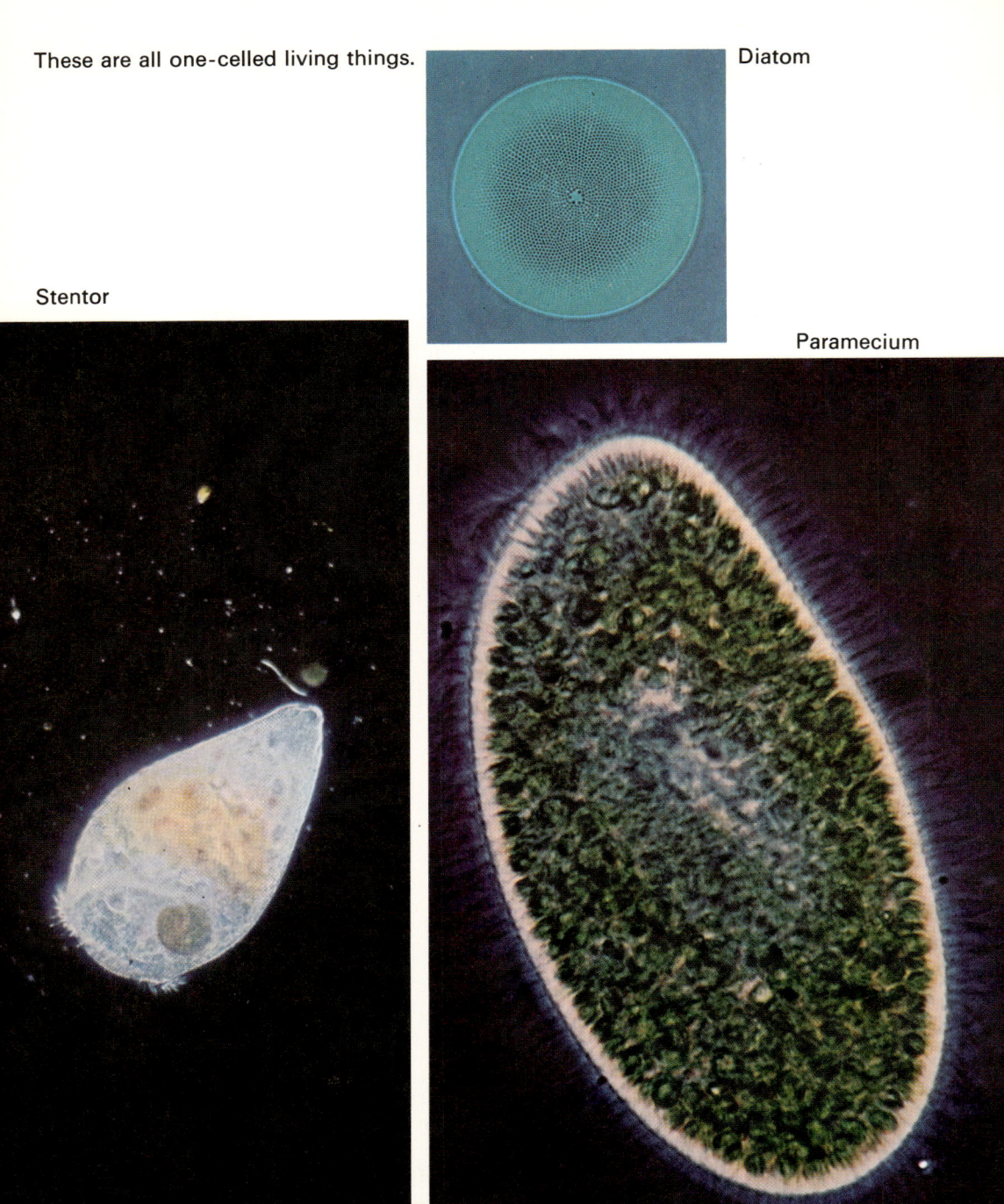

One-celled living things are very tiny plants or animals that have only a single body part. This part is the CELL.

One-celled living things and some other simple creatures reproduce by splitting into parts. Each part becomes a new living thing just like the one that split.

These paramecia are reproducing by splitting.

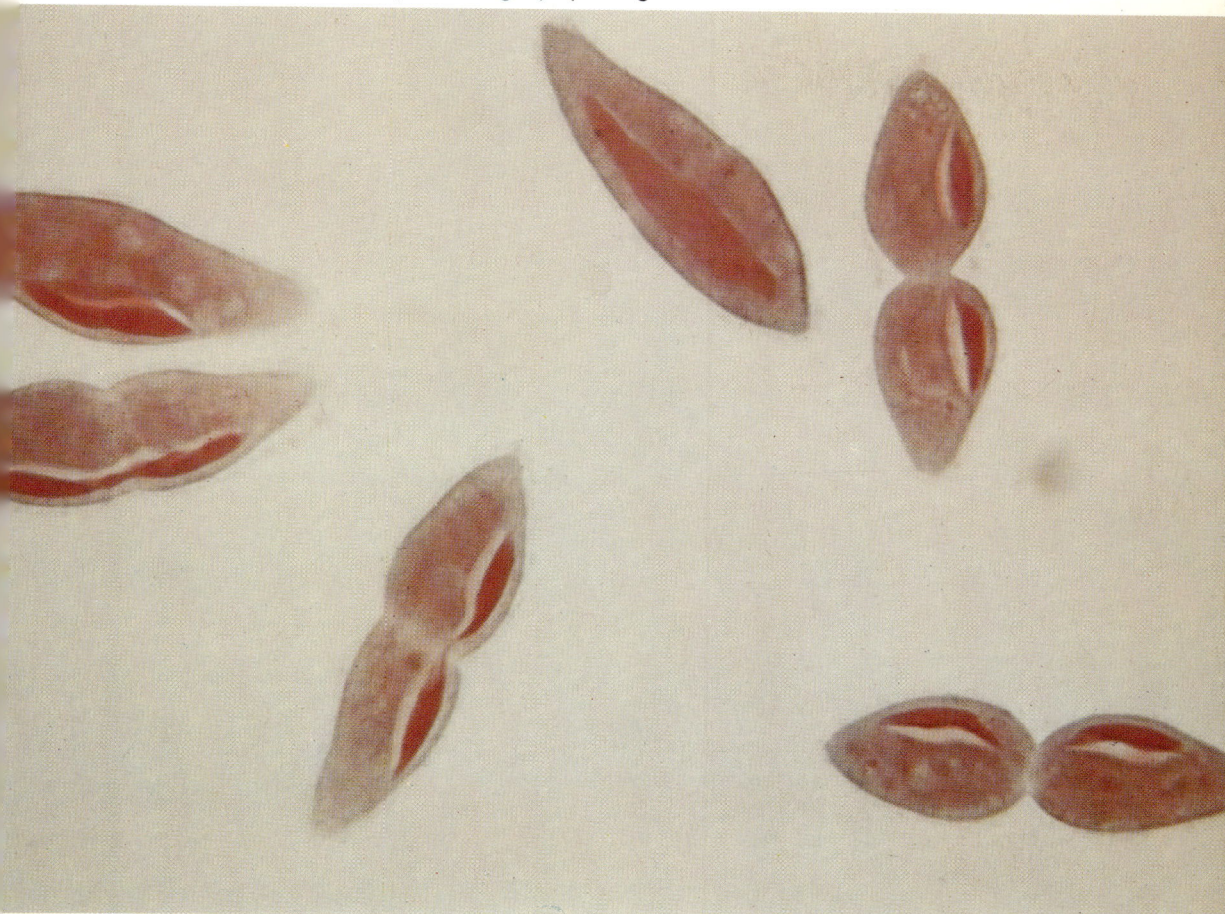

COURTESY, CCM: GENERAL BIOLOGICAL, INC., CHICAGO   WALTER DAWN

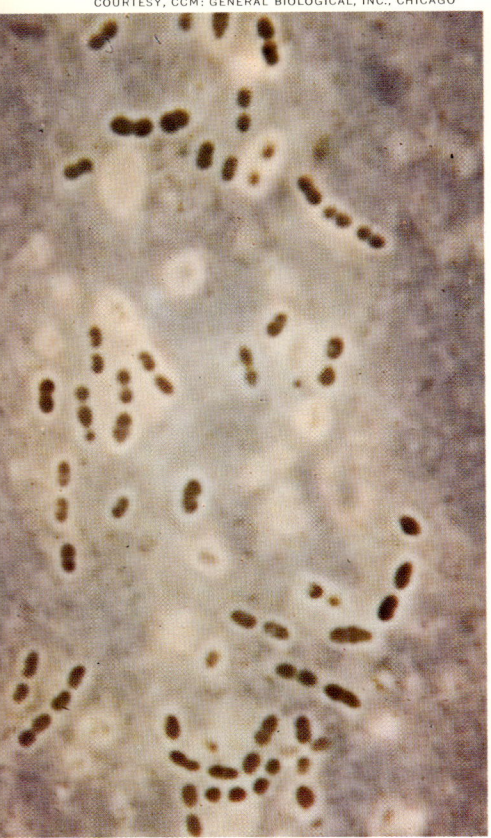

These bacteria cause the disease pneumonia.

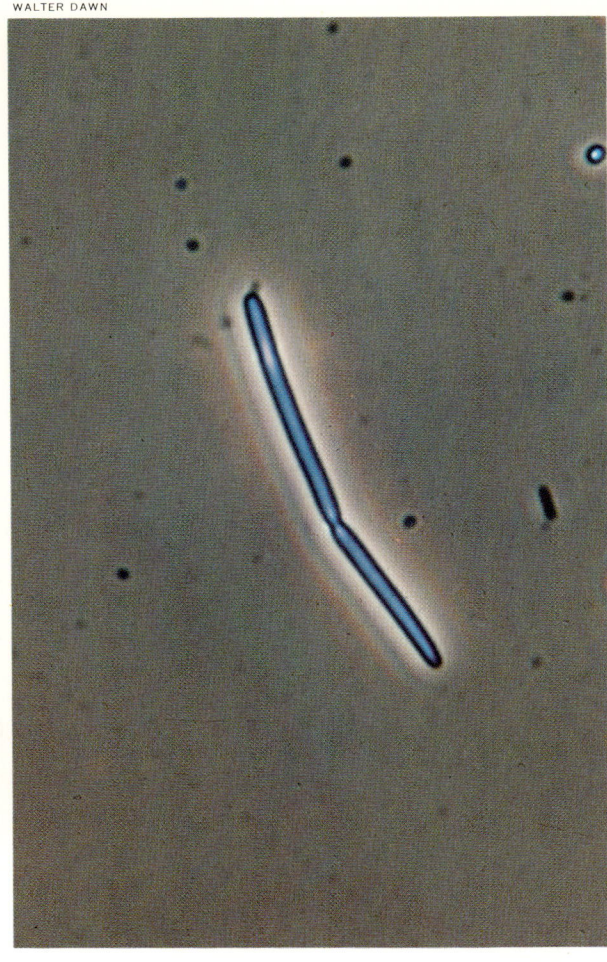

Lactobacillus: A kind of bacteria often found in milk. This one is reproducing by splitting.

Germs are one-celled living things. They reproduce by splitting again and again. This is how a few disease germs, entering our bodies, can grow into millions within a short time.

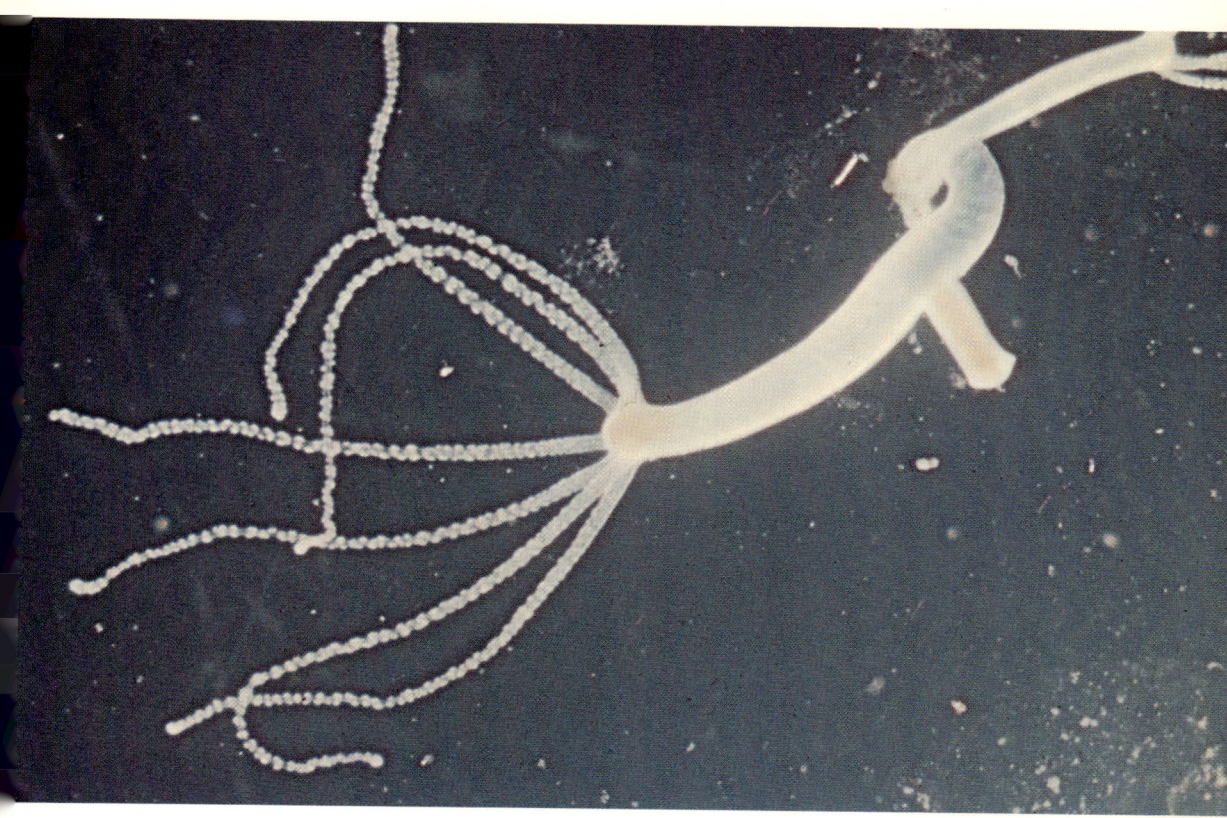

Hydra

The hydra is a small water animal with a body made of many cells. Most of the animals we know have bodies with many cells.

The hydra can reproduce by splitting in a special way. If its small body is broken apart, each part will grow into a new hydra.

This way of reproduction is something like the splitting of one-celled animals.

Sometimes a little knob will grow on one side of the hydra's body. The knob turns into a small hydra. After a time, the small hydra breaks away and goes off to live by itself.

This way of reproduction is called BUDDING.

COURTESY, CCM: GENERAL BIOLOGICAL, INC., CHICAGO

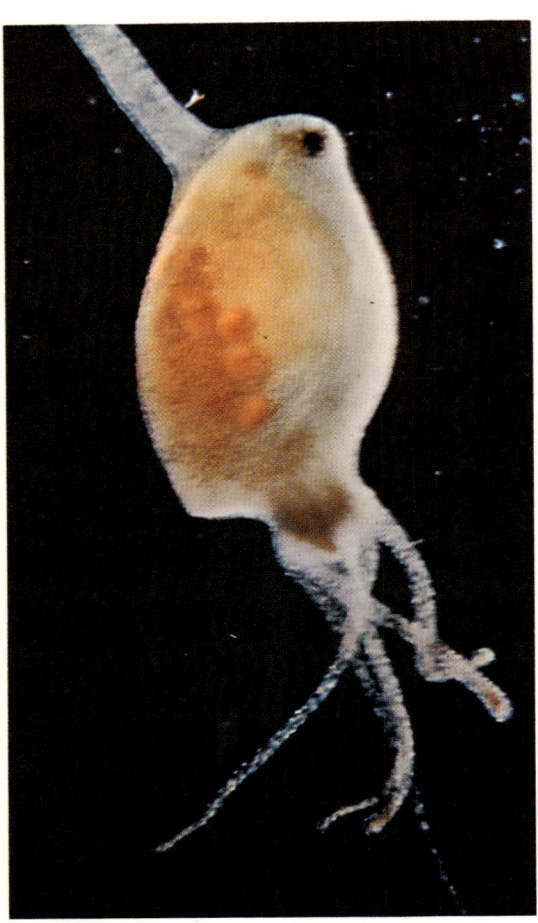

This hydra has swallowed a water flea.

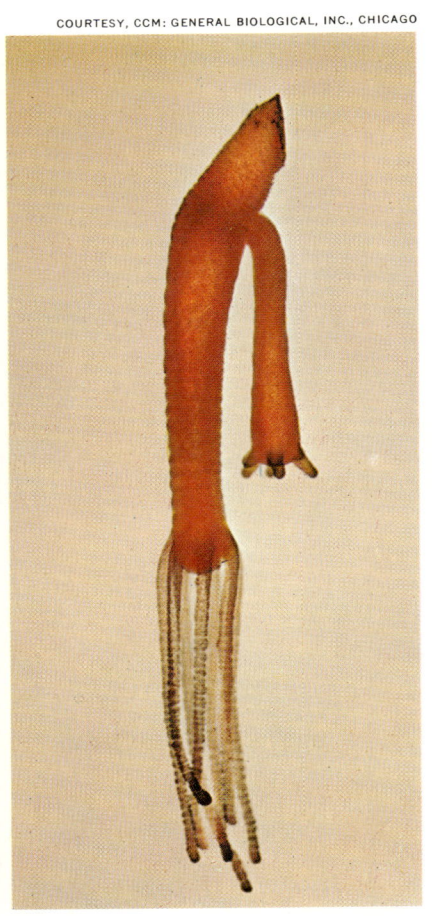

This hydra has grown a small hydra on its body. This means of reproduction is called budding. The young hydra will break off and live by itself.

The hydra can also reproduce in a third way. When the weather grows cool or the pond where the animal lives starts to dry up, the hydra makes special cells. These cells leave the hydra and go swimming in the water.

The cells are male sex cells, called SPERM CELLS.

Another part of the hydra's body makes a different kind of cell. This is the OVUM or egg cell. (The plural of ovum is OVA.)

The ova are the female sex cells. They are inside tiny prickly balls, which stay joined to the hydra.

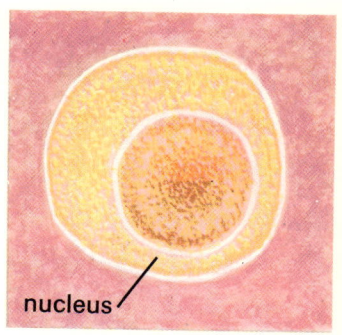

OVUM OR EGG CELL

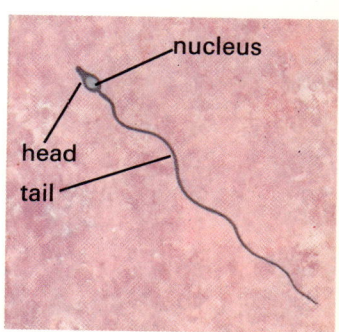

SPERM CELL

Many animals have sperm cells and ova that look like these. The sperm cell is much smaller than the ovum, and it is able to swim by means of its lashing "tail." Later, the sperm "head" and the nucleus or center of the ovum will join together to make a single fertilized cell—the beginning of the new animal.

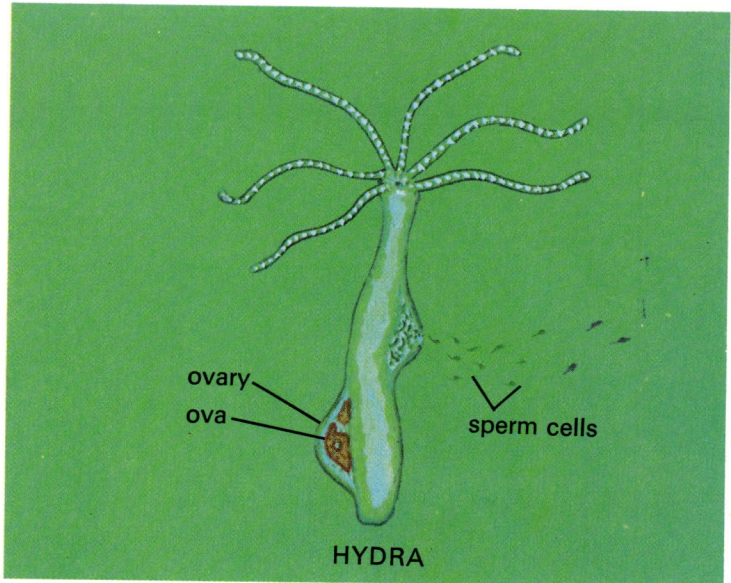

HYDRA

The hydra can produce both ova and sperm cells. The sperm cells leave the hydra and swim through the water. The ova stay attached to the hydra, inside small prickly balls called ovaries.

Hydras often live in small ponds like this one.

The many sperm cells swim around until some of them find an egg, or ovum. Then one sperm cell joins with the egg to make a new cell. When this happens, we say that the egg has been FERTILIZED.

The fertilized egg drops off the hydra and rests. It may stay buried in damp mud for many months.

When the weather becomes warm and water fills the pond again, the egg will open. A tiny new hydra, that grew from the fertilized ovum, will come out.

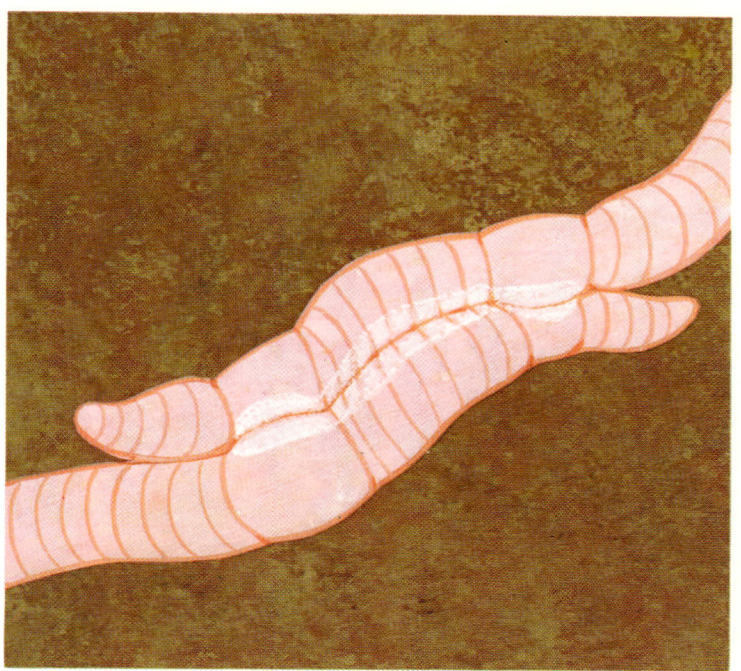

EARTHWORMS MATING
Each worm gives sperm cells to the other. Each uses the sperm cells from the other to fertilize its own eggs. The fertilized eggs are laid in a kind of cocoon in the ground. After a while, small young worms come out.

Because a hydra can reproduce by making male and female sex cells, we say it can have SEXUAL REPRODUCTION.

But there are no separate "mother" or "father" hydras. Every hydra is both a mother and a father because it makes both male and female sex cells.

The earthworm is another animal that is both male and female at the same time, because each worm makes both ova and sperm cells.

17

Most of the living things we see around us reproduce through sexual reproduction. But most of them have separate male and female animals. The same animal cannot be both at once.

The father, or male, makes the sperm cells in a body part called the TESTIS.

The mother, or female, makes the ova in a body part called the OVARY.

Adult sockeye salmon getting ready to mate. The male is the one closer to the top of the picture.

A mother and father animal must come together in a special way to reproduce. This is called MATING.

When two salmon mate, the female pours many eggs out of her body. The male swims close by and pours out a liquid called milt. The milt is full of many tiny sperm cells. Only one sperm cell can join with each ovum and fertilize it. The sperm cells and ova that do not meet will soon die.

Eggs or ova are fertilized when milt, a liquid containing sperm cells, is poured over them by the male fish.

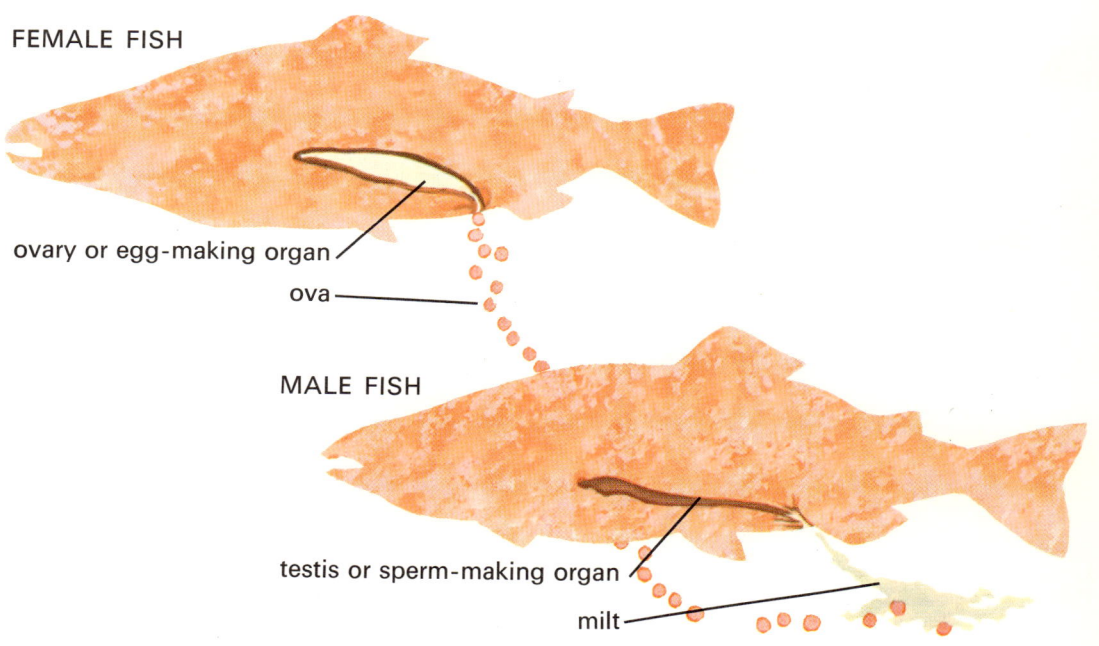

FEMALE FISH

ovary or egg-making organ

ova

MALE FISH

testis or sperm-making organ

milt

Salmon leaping upstream on the way to the place where they will mate.

Fertilized ovum

The fertilized ovum has divided in two. Now there are two smaller cells clinging together.

Each of the two cells has divided, and now there are four cells clinging together.

Each of the four cells has divided, and now there are eight smaller cells.

Each new cell has divided, and now there is a group of sixteen cells clinging together.

The cells continue to divide. Now there is a group of many cells in the shape of a hollow ball.

DEVELOPMENT OF A FERTILIZED SALMON EGG

After an egg is fertilized, the one cell divides into two parts, but the cells do not separate. Instead of one large cell, there are two smaller cells clinging together. This is something like the reproduction of one-celled living things such as germs; but the new cells stay together instead of splitting apart.

Each of these new smaller cells divides in two again. Now there are four cells in a cluster.

The four cells divide into eight, and the eight cells become sixteen. The cells divide again and again, until there is a bunch of many tiny cells, all clinging together.

The cells continue to divide. They form into a hollow ball. The hollow ball soon looks as though it had been pushed in on one end. The cells are still dividing again and again.

BILL REASONS FROM NATIONAL AUDUBON SOCIETY

If you look carefully, you can see some salmon eggs lying among the pebbles. Some of the eggs may be eaten by other animals, but the mother fish has laid thousands, so many of them will live.

The mother and father salmon have gone away. They do not help their fertilized eggs change into young salmon.

Sockeye salmon eggs after one month. The dark spots are the embryos' eyes.

After about a month, the tiny living thing inside the salmon egg has formed body parts. It is called a salmon EMBRYO. The embryo lives on nourishment contained in the egg.

The embryo has eyes and a tail. It is made of many, many thousands of cells. And new cells keep forming every day.

More than two months later, the tiny fish are ready to hatch from the eggs. When they do, they still have a bit of orange yolk joined to their bodies. This gives them food for about three months. After this time, when the yolk is all gone, the young fish catch food for themselves.

Some of the young fish may be eaten by other animals. Others will become grown-up, or adult, fish. Some will be males and others females. They will be able to mate and produce more young.

This is how young sockeye salmon look when they have just hatched. They are still tiny. The orange sacs are egg yolk.

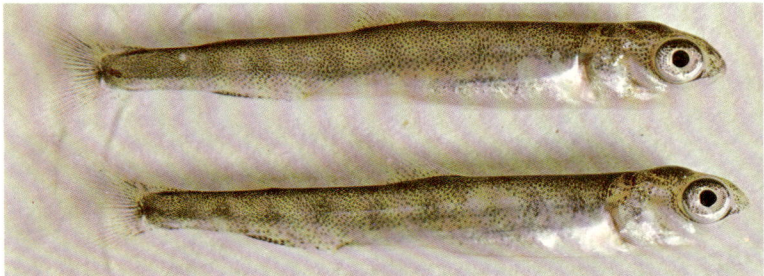

Sockeye salmon about four months after they are hatched. They are about one inch long.

Frogs and toads mate in a way that is much like the mating of fish. The male and female go to a place where there is water. The female crouches down, and the male climbs onto her back. As she lays her eggs in the water, he pours his sperm cells onto them. Only one sperm can enter each ovum and fertilize it.

The fertilized ova soon become embryos. And after about nine days the embryos become the tiny "baby" animals that we call tadpoles.

STAGES IN THE LIFE OF A FROG

1 Frogs mate when the male climbs onto the female's back. She lays eggs while he pours out sperm cells.

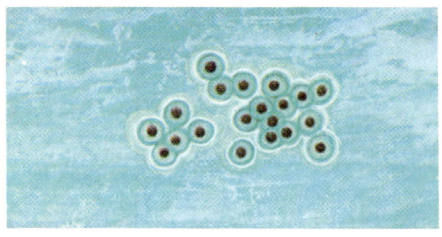

2 Fertilized frog eggs grow into embryos.

3 Tadpole develops from the embryo. It catches its own food.

4 Tadpole develops hind legs first, growing larger and larger.

5 Looking more and more like a frog, the tadpole grows front legs. Its tail gets smaller.

6 Adult frog has no tail.

Cheetah

JOHN H. GERARD FROM NATIONAL AUDUBON SOCIETY

Opossum

Palomino mare and colt

All of these animals live on land.

White-tailed deer

Ova and sperm cells are very tiny, wet living things. They cannot live in the open air. They die if they dry up. Animals that live on land cannot reproduce in the same way that water animals do. If animals poured their eggs and sperm cells onto the ground, the little sex cells would die.

The eggs of land animals are fertilized while they are still within the body of the female.

These two butterflies are mating. The male and female have joined the openings at the ends of their bodies. Sperm cells from the male butterfly will pass into the body of the female. The sperm cells will swim through the body liquids of the female until they find the ova and fertilize them.

Cabbage butterflies mating

The body of the female will make a firm, thin covering, or shell, for each fertilized ovum. The shell will keep the ovum from drying out.

The female lays her eggs on the leaves of a plant that will be good food for her young. Inside the shells, the cells will divide and embryos will form.

After a few days, the eggs will hatch. Caterpillars will come out, eat, and grow. Later they will change into chrysalises and then into butterflies.

STAGES IN THE LIFE OF A CABBAGE BUTTERFLY

Eggs

Newly hatched larva or caterpillar

Full-grown larva

Chrysalis

Butterfly coming out of chrysalis

Adult butterfly

Chicken ova have very large yellow yolks. The sex cell itself is tiny. It is attached to the surface of the yolk. A fully developed yolk moves down the tube from the ovary. It becomes surrounded by egg white and enclosed in two membranes, which are something like thin skin. The shell is formed by glands in the lower part of the tube.

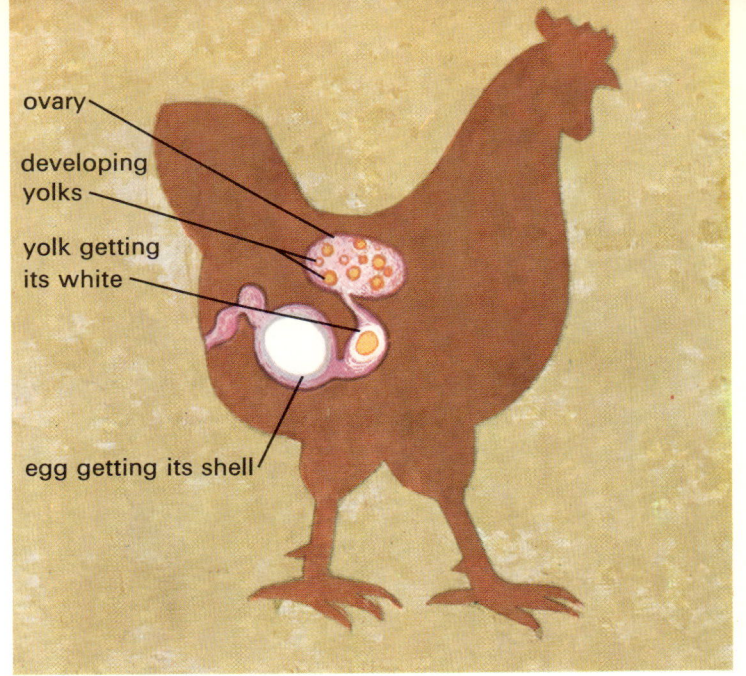

Birds lay eggs, too. Each egg contains a tiny ovum. It also contains a yolk, which provides nourishment for the embryo as it grows.

When birds are ready to mate, the male bird hops onto the back of the female. An opening in his body beneath his tail touches an opening in the female's body beneath her tail. Sperm cells pass quickly from the male's body into the body of the female.

The sperm cells meet the ova, which have not formed their shells yet. The sperm cells fertilize the ova.

Later, the ova move through the body of the female and get their whites and shells. The eggs are laid through the same opening that the sperm cells entered.

Goldfinch babies are quite helpless when they hatch. The mother bird must feed and care for them.

These baby chicks are able to run about and feed themselves soon after they hatch.

The female bird sits on the eggs in the nest. She must keep them warm while the embryos form inside. Fertilized chicken eggs hatch in about 21 days.

Baby chicks can run about at once and feed themselves. Other baby birds, such as robins, are helpless when they hatch. The robin parents must feed their babies and care for them until they are able to live alone.

Many reptiles also lay eggs with shells containing an ovum and a yolk for nourishment. Eggs with shells are much safer from harm than soft eggs laid in the water. But there are still many things that can happen to them.

Many animals use other animals' eggs for food. Sometimes the eggs are destroyed by accident. And if the eggs are not kept warm, they may not hatch.

LYNWOOD M. CHACE FROM NATIONAL AUDUBON SOCIETY

This snapping turtle mother is laying her eggs in a hole she has made in the sand. The sun will warm the eggs. Newly hatched turtles can care for themselves.

When snakes mate, the male and female twine around each other, joining the openings on the lower sides of their bodies, near the end of the tail. Sperm cells from the male pass into the body of the female.

Some snakes lay eggs with leathery shells. But other kinds do not lay their eggs. Instead, the eggs hatch within the mother's body and the baby snakes are born alive.

This black racer snake lays her eggs in the woods. The eggs are kept warm by the sun. The mother snake does not take care of them. After about ten weeks, the baby snakes hatch from the eggs and begin to catch their own food.

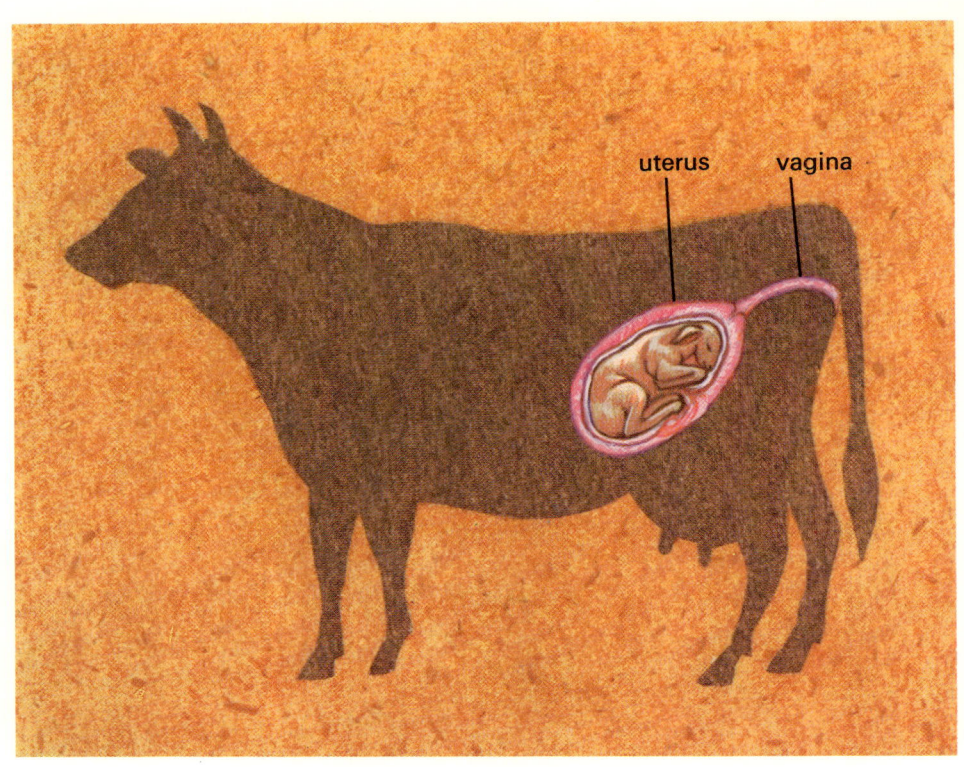

This calf will develop inside its mother's body.

Mammals are animals with fur or hair. Squirrels, elephants, deer, lions, monkeys, and people are all mammals. Mammals have a different way of reproducing.

Most mammal ova are very, very tiny and have no shells. The ova of these mammals are fertilized inside the body of the mother, but they are not laid outside at all. Instead, the fertilized eggs stay inside the mother's body, and the young animals grow safely within her.

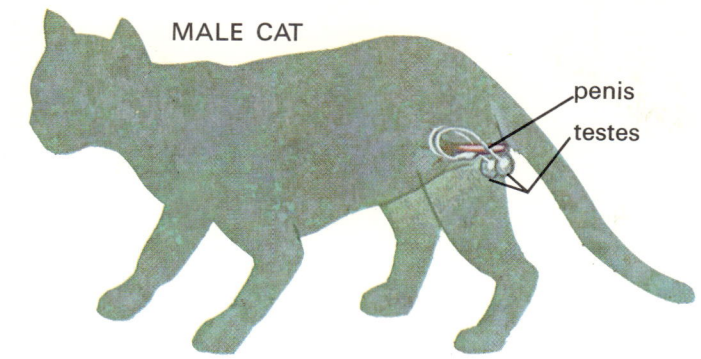

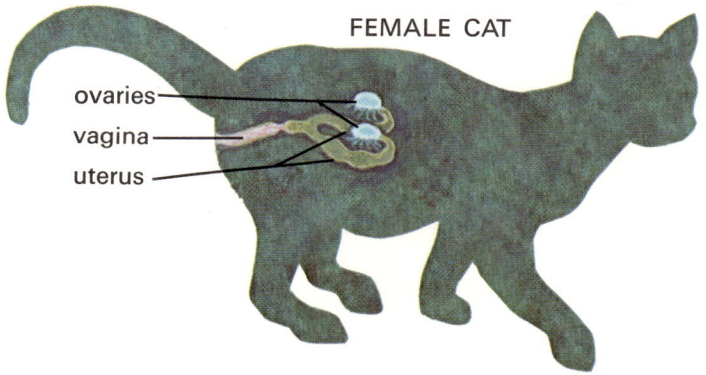

A female mammal, like this mother cat, has two ovaries that make tiny ova. The father cat has two testes that make sperm cells.

When cats are ready to mate, they call to each other by growling, whining, and meowing. They may pretend to fight. These acts are known as COURTSHIP. Different animals have different ways of courtship, or preparing to mate.

When the cats are ready to mate, the male climbs onto the female's back. He has a body part called the PENIS which is shaped something like a tube. He slips his penis into a special opening in the body of the female cat below her tail. Sperm cells pass from the penis into the opening which is called the VAGINA. This passage is also called the BIRTH CANAL.

Some of the sperm cells swim on and meet ova. A few ova are fertilized. Only one sperm cell can fertilize each ovum. The fertilized ova move into a hollow organ called the UTERUS in the female's body. The fertilized ova become attached to the walls of the uterus and start to grow.

Kitten embryos are developing inside the mother cat's uterus.

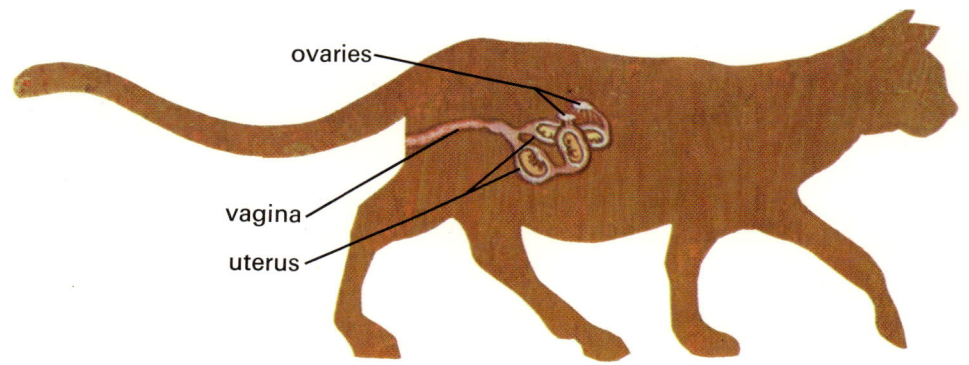

Each fertilized ovum divides into two cells, and each new cell divides again. The cells keep on dividing as the new living things develop inside the mother cat's uterus. After a time, each little group of cells becomes an embryo.

The cat embryos grow larger and larger. They grow legs and ears and fur. They get claws and even whiskers. A cord leads from the belly of each kitten to the wall of the uterus. The unborn kittens do not have to eat or breathe. Blood flowing through their cords brings all that they need to live and grow. They are safe and warm inside their mother's body.

The baby kittens have grown. They are almost ready to be born.

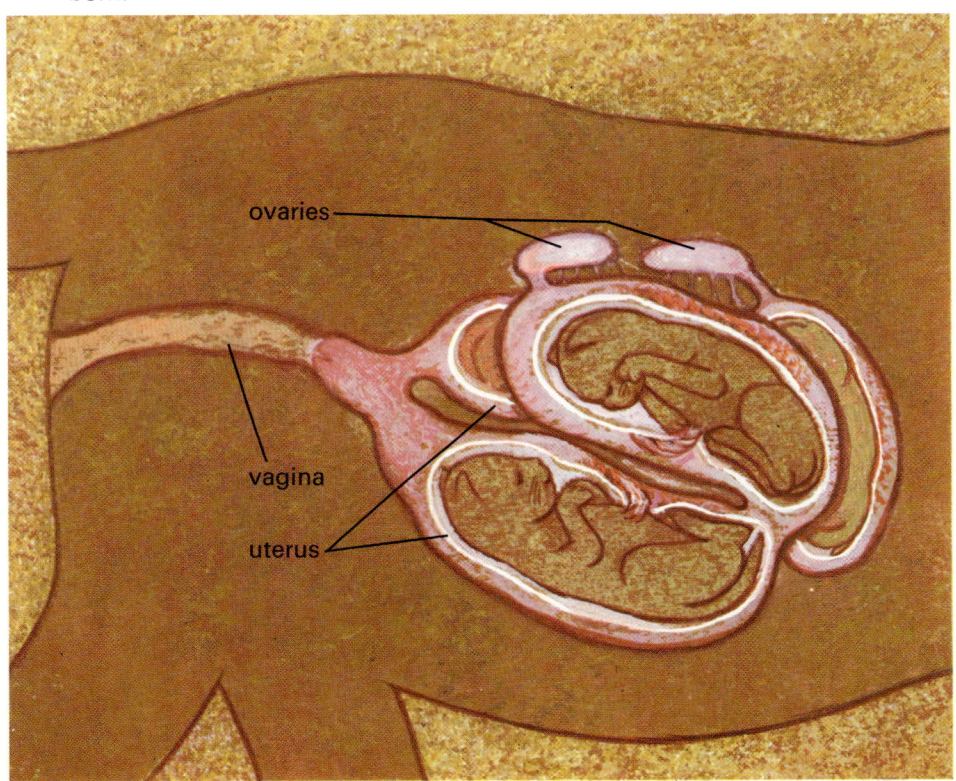

When a kitten is born, the mother cat bites through the cord, and licks her kitten clean.

After about 63 days, the kittens are ready to be born. The muscles in the uterus begin to squeeze and push. The kittens move through the vagina, or birth canal, which stretches to let them through. They come out through the opening below the mother's tail where the sperm cells entered.

The mother cat licks her babies' bellies to help them start to breathe. She bites through the cords, which are no longer needed. After all her kittens are born and washed, she helps them to eat.

When they have all been born, she helps them to nurse.

Each mother mammal has body parts, the BREASTS, that make milk. All newborn mammals must nurse, or drink milk. The new kittens push their little faces into the fur of their mother's belly. They find nipples there. They drink until they can hold no more, and then they sleep.

The mother cat will care for her babies for about eight weeks. She will nurse them, keep them clean, and teach them how to take care of themselves.

Some mammals have several young at one time. Other mammals, such as horses and human beings, usually have only one baby at a time. The number of babies usually depends on the number of ova given off by the mother's ovaries at one time.

All baby mammals are born because their parents mated. Every mammal baby has both a mother and a father, because both male and female cells are needed to form an embryo.

All baby animals will grow up to be the same kind of animals as their parents. A mother cat will give birth to kittens, not puppies. A mother rabbit will have baby rabbits, not baby mice or baby cats.

Bison

Mammal babies cannot take care of themselves right after they are born in the way that young fish and reptiles can. The mother—and sometimes the father, too—must care for them.

Besides feeding the babies, the parents must shelter them from cold and dampness, and guard them from harm. The parents must teach their young how to find food and how to avoid danger.

These mother animals carry their babies to protect them from harm. It does not hurt the tiger cub to be carried by the skin of its neck.

Tiger

Baboon

Porpoises are mammals. The baby porpoise grows in its mother's uterus and is born alive like other mammals. It emerges from the uterus tail first. The mother pushes the baby to the surface of the water so that it can breathe air. The young porpoise will stay with its mother and learn from her.

The most intelligent kinds of animals care for and teach their babies the longest. A young porpoise swims with its mother for about six years. A young ape stays with its mother as long as eight or nine years.

Lion cub nursing

After the young animals have learned all they can from their parents, they are ready to live alone. When they are adults, they will look for mates. They do not have to learn to do this. A very strong feeling, called a mating INSTINCT, leads animals to mate.

Another instinct leads animals to care for their young. Scientists do not believe that animals feel true love for their mates or babies in the way that human beings do. What seems like the love of a mother animal for her baby is really instinct. Animals take care of their young, just as they breathe and sleep, without having to learn how or think about it.

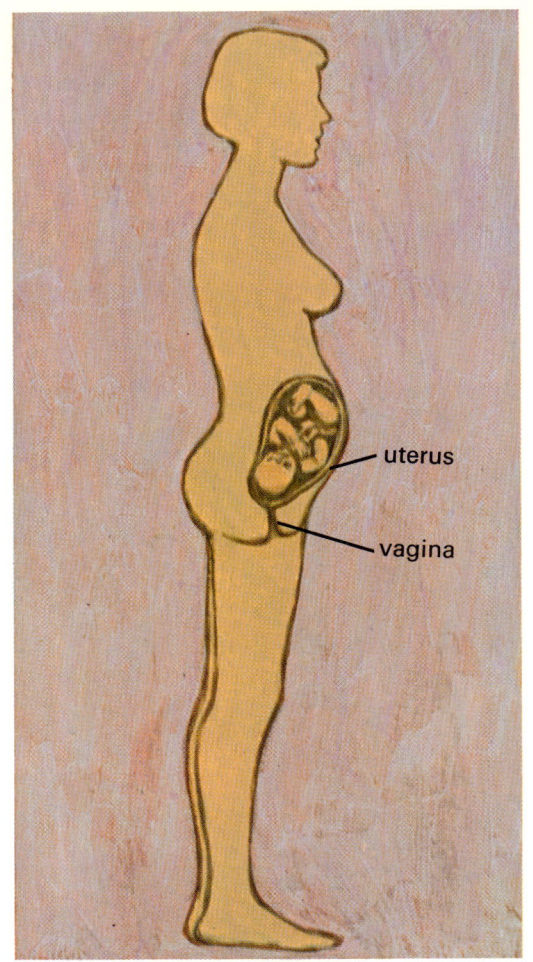

A human baby develops inside its mother's uterus.

Human beings are mammals, too. Every human baby begins its life as a tiny fertilized ovum inside its mother's body. The fertilized ovum divides again and again as it moves along toward the uterus. It settles there and begins to form an embryo.

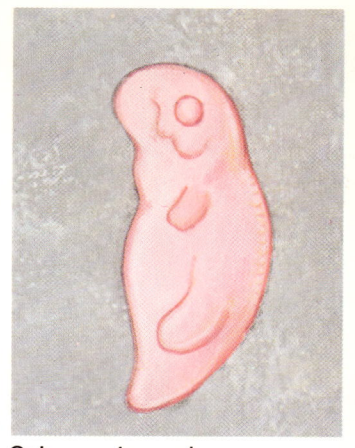
Salamander embryo

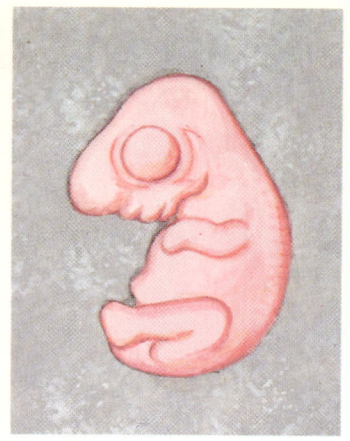
Blackbird embryo

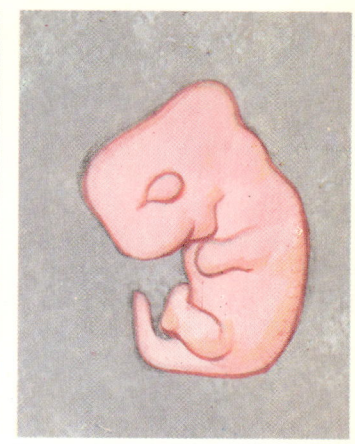
Rat embryo

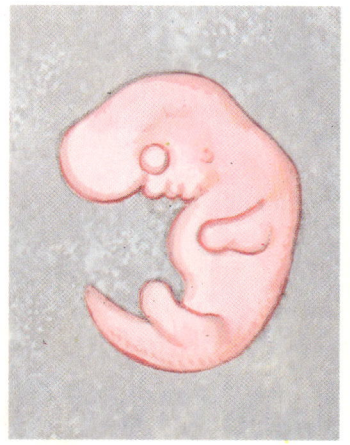
Rabbit embryo

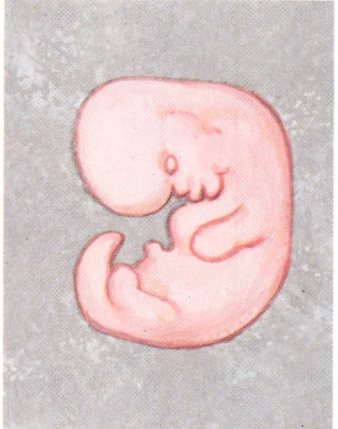
Human embryo

At first, a human embryo looks much like the embryos of fish, reptiles, birds, and other mammals. But it does not look like these animals for long. It changes.

A human baby grows inside its mother's uterus until it is born. When it is born, it needs to be cared for because it is helpless.

Human parents care for their children because of love, not just instinct. They want to do it. This is one of the most important ways that people are different from other forms of animal life.

Glossary

BREAST (*brest*) A gland located on the upper chest of humans and some other mammals. In the female, the breasts produce milk shortly after the birth of a baby.

BUDDING (*BUD-ing*) A reproductive process in lower animals in which a new individual develops from a "bud" or bulge on the body wall of an adult animal.

CELL (*sel*) The smallest unit of plant or animal bodies. A cell is often a microscopic bit of living material with a specialized function. The simplest plants and animals have bodies consisting of a single cell.

COURTSHIP (*KORT-ship*) Activities which take place between a male and a female animal before mating.

EGG (*eg*) The female sex cell or ovum, especially an ovum having a rather firm outer coat or shell.

EMBRYO (*EM-bree-oh*) A plant or animal in a very early stage of development. In humans, the developing baby from the time of its implantation in the wall of the uterus (about two weeks after conception) until near the end of the second month of development, after which it is called a FETUS.

FERTILIZATION (*FUR-tuh-luh-ZAY-shun*) The union of the male and female sex cells; conception.

INSTINCT (*IN-stinkt*) An inherited pattern of behavior.

MAMMAL (*MAM-ul*) A member of the highest group of animals with backbones. Mammals have hair or fur, and feed their young with milk, a nourishing fluid produced by mammary glands (called breasts in humans and some other animals).

MATING (*MAY-ting*) The coming together of a male and female animal for the purpose of reproduction.

OVARY (*OH-vuh-ree*) An organ which produces and stores ova, or eggs. In the human female, one of two glands about the size and shape of almonds, located within the abdomen.

OVUM (*OH-vum*) Plural: OVA (*OH-vuh*) A female sex cell, or egg.

PENIS (*PEE-nus*) The male sex organ through which sperm cells pass out of the body. It is used for introducing sperm cells into the vagina of the female. In humans, the penis is located at the lower front of the male abdomen.

REPRODUCE (*ree-pro-DOOS*) To have young or babies.

SEXUAL REPRODUCTION (*SEK-shoo-ul ree-pro-DUK-shun*) One way of reproducing, in which a female sex cell and a male sex cell unite to form a new individual.

SPERM CELL (*spurm sel*) A male sex cell. Its scientific name is SPERMATOZOON (plural: SPERMATOZOA) but it is often spoken of as a SPERM.

TESTIS (*TESS-tus*) Plural: TESTES (*TESS-teez*) An organ which produces sperm cells. The human testes, often called TESTICLES, are two glands about the size and shape of almonds contained within a sac of skin, the SCROTUM, at the lower front of the male abdomen just behind the penis.

UTERUS (*YOO-ter-us*) A hollow organ in which the fertilized ovum embeds itself and develops before birth. In humans, a pear-shaped organ normally about the size of a clenched fist located within the lower abdomen of the female. Also called the WOMB.

VAGINA (*vuh-JY-nuh*) The passageway in the female body in which sperm cells are deposited by the male's penis. The vagina leads to the uterus, It is also called the BIRTH CANAL, since the young pass through it at the time of birth.